SPECIAL REPORTS

THE IMPEACHMENT OF
DONALD TRUMP

BY SUE BRADFORD EDWARDS

CONTENT CONSULTANT
ROBERT Y. SHAPIRO, PhD
PROFESSOR OF POLITICAL SCIENCE AND
INTERNATIONAL AND PUBLIC AFFAIRS
COLUMBIA UNIVERSITY

Essential Library
An Imprint of Abdo Publishing | abdobooks.com

abdobooks.com

Published by Abdo Publishing, a division of ABDO, PO Box 398166, Minneapolis,
Minnesota 55439. Copyright © 2021 by Abdo Consulting Group, Inc. International
copyrights reserved in all countries. No part of this book may be reproduced in
any form without written permission from the publisher. Essential Library™ is a
trademark and logo of Abdo Publishing.

Printed in the United States of America, North Mankato, Minnesota.
062020
092020

**THIS BOOK CONTAINS
RECYCLED MATERIALS**

Cover Photo: Michael Brochstein/Sipa USA/AP Images
Interior Photos: Patrick Semansky/AP Images, 4–5, 9, 59; Pat Benic/
picture-alliance/dpa/AP Images, 7; Bill Clark/CQ Roll Call/AP Images, 11; Alex
Brandon/AP Images, 16–17, 68; Everett Historical/Shutterstock Images, 19; AP
Images, 23; Manuel Balce Ceneta/AP Images, 27; Paul Holston/AP Images, 28–29;
J. Scott Applewhite/AP Images, 31, 52–53, 74–75, 82–83; John Locher/AP
Images, 32; Pavlo Gonchar/SOPA Images/Sipa USA/AP Images, 40–41; Nick Wass/
AP Images, 44; Red Line Editorial, 47, 90–91; Andrew Harnik/AP Images, 62–63;
Senate Television/AP Images, 77; Rod Lamkey Jr./SIPA USA/AP Images, 81; Caroline
Brehman/CQ Roll Call/AP Images, 86; Yuri Gripas/Abaca/Sipa USA/AP Images,
92–93; Tom Williams/CQ Roll Call/AP Images, 95; Michael Brochstein/Sipa USA/AP
Images, 99

Editor: Charly Haley
Series Designer: Maggie Villaume

Library of Congress Control Number: 2020935592

Publisher's Cataloging-in-Publication Data

Names: Edwards, Sue Bradford, author.
Title: The impeachment of Donald Trump / by Sue Bradford Edwards
Description: Minneapolis, Minnesota : Abdo Publishing, 2021 | Series: Special reports
    | Includes online resources and index
Identifiers: ISBN 9781532194016 (lib. bdg.) | ISBN 9781098212858 (ebook)
Subjects: LCSH: Presidents--Juvenile literature. | Trump, Donald, 1946---Juvenile
    literature. | Obstruction of justice--Juvenile literature. | Impeachment--
    Juvenile literature.
Classification: DDC 342.73062--dc23

CONTENTS

CHAPTER ONE

"LET US IN!"

O n the morning of October 23, 2019, members of the US House of Representatives' Oversight Committee, Foreign Affairs Committee, and Intelligence Committee assembled for a meeting. They had gathered in the SCIF, or sensitive compartmented information facility, a room specifically designed for meetings in which top secret information might be discussed. The committee members were there to hear the deposition of Laura Cooper, the US government's deputy assistant defense secretary for Russia, Ukraine, and Eurasia. Her sworn testimony would help determine whether the House of Representatives would make the decision to impeach President Donald Trump.

House Minority Whip Steve Scalise, backed by several other Republican representatives, speaks at a news conference asking for access to the closed-door meeting.

President Trump was accused of asking the president of Ukraine, Volodymyr Zelensky, over the phone to investigate the son of Trump's political rival, former US vice president and 2020 presidential candidate Joe Biden. In July 2019, at the time of the phone call, Biden was a strong candidate for Democratic presidential nominee, Trump's chief rival in the upcoming presidential election. An investigation would call Biden's character into question and could cost him votes. Trump had allegedly made this request to Zelensky after blocking military aid to Ukraine and making it clear that the aid would be released once the investigation began. Members of the House of Representatives were holding hearings to see whether they could find evidence to support these accusations.

SCIF

A SCIF (pronounced "skiff") is a secure space that is designed to be spy-proof. The design of an individual facility depends on how that SCIF will be used. Some are storerooms housing sensitive data. Others are meeting rooms where sensitive topics can be discussed. In a meeting room, special shielding prevents radio signals from being transmitted or received by anyone in the room. The walls and ceiling are insulated and sealed to keep sounds, such as people speaking, from being heard on the outside. These rooms give government representatives places to safely discuss top secret information.

President Trump, *left*, shakes hands with Vice President Biden, *right*, and President Barack Obama, *center*, at Trump's inauguration ceremony in 2017.

Cooper had taken her seat but had not started speaking when three doors leading into the room burst open. A crowd of more than 30 people entered the room shouting, "Let us in!"[1] Representative Gerry Connolly, a Democrat from Virginia, was attending the meeting. He later said the group seemed aggressive and potentially threatening.

It took a moment for everyone attending the meeting to realize what was happening. Then they

"BREAKING: I LED OVER 30 OF MY COLLEAGUES INTO THE SCIF WHERE ADAM SCHIFF IS HOLDING SECRET IMPEACHMENT DEPOSITIONS. STILL INSIDE – MORE DETAILS TO COME."[2]

—TWEET FROM REPRESENTATIVE MATT GAETZ, REPUBLICAN FROM FLORIDA, OCTOBER 23, 2019

recognized that the entering group was composed of fellow representatives, all Republicans. Two of the Republican representatives, Bradley Byrne from Alabama and Louie Gohmert from Texas, yelled about the unfairness of the hearing process. Val Demings, a Democrat representing Florida, shouted back at Gohmert and Byrne, demanding to know whether Republicans were trying to teach their children "that it's OK to lie, steal, and cheat so long as you don't get caught?" To another Republican she said, "Don't you have any work to do today?"[3]

Representative Adam Schiff, chairman of the House Intelligence Committee and a California Democrat, was in charge of the meeting. He asked the group of Republican representatives to leave. The group members refused, stating they were there to protest secret meetings like this one. Because the room was no longer secure, Cooper could not give her deposition. She departed until the meeting could resume.

Schiff said the meetings were not secret. Attendance is limited to members of the committees holding the meetings. Several of the protesting representatives

Cooper walks by security guards on her way to testify before House committee members in the SCIF.

would have been able to attend the meeting normally if they had wanted to, since they were members of the relevant committees. Schiff also said typed transcripts of the meeting would be made public at a later date. The Republican protesters did not leave.

By rule, those using the SCIF are expected to leave their cell phones at the door. "All of us put our electronics in boxes outside," Connolly said. "That SCIF is used by Congress for lots of highly classified purposes."[4] When asked to comply with this rule, some of the Republicans surrendered their phones. The group settled in, some having snacks and pizza delivered. Eventually they left,

NO PHONES ALLOWED

Not only does a SCIF need to be made secure when it is built but it also needs to be kept secure, which limits what people can bring into or take out of the room. Devices that can transmit or receive information over radio frequencies, including anything with Bluetooth, are forbidden. Other banned items include electronics that can take photographs, record video, or record audio. Cell phones cannot be taken into a SCIF because they have all these capabilities and more. Malware, or malicious software, can be installed on a cell phone. Through malware someone can control the phone and use it to record what is happening in a SCIF or anywhere else without the owner of the phone knowing.

at about two o'clock that afternoon, so they could participate in several House votes on other issues. But even then, the meeting could not resume. The House sergeant at arms, a law enforcement official who serves in the Capitol, had to come to the SCIF and sweep the room for surveillance devices to ensure it was still secure. The meeting started at three, and Cooper was allowed to give her statement.

HOUSE RULES

The Republican protesters told reporters that they took action and forced their way into the hearing to stand up for US voters. They said the hearings should not have taken place behind closed doors. For his part, Schiff defended this closed-door meeting, explaining that important hearings such as those that might lead to an impeachment are often held in private. He told reporters that limiting

who is in attendance keeps witnesses from listening to

each other's testimonies and altering what they plan to say

or perhaps even fabricating a story.

These rules and procedures are long-standing,

including asking someone to leave a hearing. "House rules

and committee rules allow the Intel Committee to close

Representative Louie Gohmert was among the Republicans who entered the
SCIF during the closed-door meeting on October 23, 2019.

hearings and other meetings behind closed doors," said George Washington University political science professor Sarah Binder. "The House—and its committees—adopt their rules by majority vote at the start of each Congress."[5] The rules governing these closed-door hearings were established before any hearings into President Trump and his phone calls with the Ukrainian president.

Chris Stewart, a Republican from Utah, participated in the protest. However, he admitted to reporters that he and the other protesters knew Schiff was following the rules. "This may be within House rules. That's not the question. The question is, is it a good idea to impeach the president in secret hearings?" Stewart said. "This may very well be within Chairman Schiff's and [Speaker of the House] Nancy Pelosi's authority to do this. I think it's a bad idea."[6] The dispute about the hearing may have lain less with established rules and regulations and more with political aims.

PARTISAN POLITICS

Although there are several political parties in the United States, the Democrats and the Republicans are the only

MORE TO THE
STORY

BENGHAZI: A CLOSED-DOOR HEARING

Closed-door House committee hearings had been used long before the investigation of President Trump. The same standard procedures were used in the Benghazi hearings investigating former secretary of state Hillary Clinton between 2014 and 2016. That investigation concerned a 2012 terrorist attack against two US government facilities in Benghazi, Libya. Four Americans died in the attacks. A House Select Committee formed to investigate whether Clinton had neglected warning signs or could have done something that would have saved these peoples' lives. As is standard practice, hearings were closed, with only committee members and witnesses present. At one point, Representative Darrell Issa, a Republican representing California, tried to enter the hearing. He was the former chairman of the Oversight Committee, but since he was no longer chairman or a member of the committee, his entrance was blocked by fellow Republican representative Trey Gowdy of South Carolina, the chairman of the committee. In this case, both Issa and Gowdy were Republicans.

two parties with substantial power. Generally, a politician who is a member of one of these parties will support what is called the party platform, a document that lays out the party's key beliefs and corresponding proposals on issues such as immigration, civil rights, and international diplomacy. Unquestioning support of a group such as a political party is called being partisan.

Politicians in federal government are often reluctant to cross party lines to work together to get an important law passed. News stories state Trump's presidency has seen a divide between parties stronger than before, although it seems impossible for the country to be more divided than it was during the American Civil War (1861–1865), when political differences literally split the country and led to war. While that level of violent division is not present today, partisan politics has increased dramatically in the years leading up to and during Trump's presidency. Division between political parties has made it difficult for members of Congress to work together to solve problems. Party support is so strong that it is often possible to predict the outcome of votes on significant issues, such as whether to investigate or impeach a president, simply by knowing how many Republicans and Democrats will vote.

The impeachment process in Trump's case was highly partisan. Democrats and Republicans, for the most part, supported their own parties. The House, with a majority of Democrats, impeached President Trump. And the Senate, with a majority of Republicans, acquitted the Republican president.

THE PARTY PERSPECTIVES

Members of the Democratic Party and the Republican Party had different viewpoints on Trump's impeachment. Most Democrats thought that it was justified for a few reasons. First, they believed Trump attempted to interfere in the next presidential election by undermining Biden, his leading political opponent. They contended that he asked a foreign power to interfere on his behalf. Second, he allegedly undermined the US Constitution by blocking House requests for information. Most Republicans believe the impeachment was wrong because, they said, the Democrats were trying to undo the will of the American people who elected President Trump. The Republicans also saw the impeachment as a Democratic abuse of power with their House majority, denying a Republican president his legal rights.

CHAPTER TWO

WHAT IS
IMPEACHMENT?

T here are many checks and balances in the US government designed to avoid abuse of power. The basis of this system is the division of government into three branches: the executive branch (or presidency), the legislative branch (or Congress), and the judicial branch (or court system). Because each branch holds part but not all of the government's power, it is difficult for one person or a small group of people to form the kind of oppressive government that led the United States to seek independence in the first place.

Impeachment is one of the checks and balances that aims to keep a political figure from abusing his or her power. It is a tool wielded by Congress to help

As President Trump delivers his State of the Union speech to Congress in February 2020, Speaker of the House Nancy Pelosi sits to his left, alongside Vice President Mike Pence to his right.

keep federal officials in check. Although impeachment is generally discussed in relation to the president, any federal official can be impeached. The first official to face impeachment was Senator William Blount in 1797.

The most severe outcome of impeachment is removal from office. But not all impeachments reach this point. In an impeachment, the House of Representatives holds a series of hearings to review evidence and then decides what charges, if any, will be made. An official who has been charged through this process has been impeached but still holds his or her office. The Senate then conducts a trial and votes on whether the official is guilty or not guilty. If a majority of senators vote

SENATOR BLOUNT

Senator William Blount (1749-1800) was one of the signers of the Constitution, but this distinction didn't protect him when his conspiracy with the British Crown was uncovered. One of Tennessee's first two senators, he was also a landowner and wanted to make sure that his property retained its value. If Spain gave its lands in modern Florida and Louisiana to France, Blount and others believed land values would drop. Because of this, they secretly worked for the land to be given to Great Britain, but their plot was uncovered. Before the House drew up Blount's articles of impeachment, the Senate voted 25 to 1 to expel him from office. The House drew up articles of impeachment, but before the case could be heard by the Senate, Blount had returned to his home state, where he was elected to the Tennessee Senate. The US Senate voted that an expelled official could be impeached, but the case was later dismissed. In spite of this, Blount was impeached by the House, and his name is first on the list of impeached US officials.

William Blount, the first US official to be impeached, served in the US Senate from 1796 to 1797.

that the official is guilty, he or she may be removed from office. Regardless of what the Senate decides, if the House votes to impeach and draws up charges against an official, this person has been impeached. A total of 20 federal government officials have been impeached by the House and tried by the Senate.[1] Of these, eight were found guilty and removed from office, and three more resigned before being convicted or acquitted.

IMPEACHMENT IN THE CONSTITUTION

When the founders of the United States wrote the Constitution, they already knew about impeachment as a tool occasionally used by the British Parliament. They wanted to make this same power available to the US Congress. According to the Constitution, the House has "the sole Power of Impeachment," meaning that it decides when an official will be charged and what the charges will be. The Constitution also states that the Senate "has the sole Power to try all Impeachments" and that a two-thirds majority is required to convict the person being tried.[2]

The Constitution lists the offenses for which someone can be impeached as "treason, bribery, or other high crimes and misdemeanors."[3] The *New York Times* approached a group of experts on constitutional law and asked them to define these terms more specifically. These experts explained that the Constitution defines *treason* as taking part in war against the United States or aiding an enemy. At the time the Constitution was written, *bribery* was understood to be when someone benefits personally from an official act. This could mean that a lawyer offers money to a judge to sway his or her decision or that a judge asks for money to rule a particular way on a case. The phrase "other high crimes and misdemeanors" means anything that works against the government or works against the good of the American people.

Even with these explanations, the list of offenses can seem vague and nonspecific. But a 1974 memo written by the House Judiciary Committee explained that it isn't the specific behavior of the president that is important. What is important is the impact this behavior has on the functioning of the US government. For example, US presidents often work closely with foreign powers to cement trade agreements, settle disputes, or fight widespread diseases. In terms of impeachment, an interaction with a foreign power alone is not the matter in question. What matters is the impact the interaction has on the US government and the American people.

IMPEACHMENTS OF THE PAST

Trump is not the only president to face impeachment. He shares this experience with Andrew Johnson, who was impeached in 1868, and Bill Clinton, who was impeached in 1998. The impeachment process began against Richard Nixon, but he resigned before the House formally voted to impeach him. Like Trump, Johnson and Clinton were both impeached but not convicted.

President Johnson, who had been Abraham Lincoln's vice president, took office on April 15, 1865, the day that President Lincoln died after being shot in an assassination. Johnson had been the US vice president during the Civil War. The Civil War was fought to force the Southern states, which had seceded to become the Confederate States of America, back into the Union, or the Northern United States. The war also ended the enslavement of African Americans. Though Johnson officially supported the North, he was born in the Confederate state of North Carolina and was sympathetic toward white Southern people. Because of this, Johnson repeatedly blocked the enforcement of laws that would empower freed slaves, such as legislation that would give them the ability to vote. He also failed to prevent white Southern rebels from regaining power in their state governments.

Then the Tenure of Office Act was passed in 1867. This law required the president to get approval from the Senate before appointing or dismissing high-ranking government officials. Johnson dismissed Secretary of War Edwin M. Stanton, Congress restored Stanton to his position, and then Johnson dismissed him again. In response, the House passed articles of impeachment against Johnson.

Richard Nixon was president from 1969 to 1974.

President Richard Nixon's troubles began with a June 17, 1972, burglary at the Democratic National Committee (DNC) headquarters at the Watergate hotel and office complex in Washington, DC. The intruders were attempting to plant electronic equipment to secretly monitor the committee's offices. Although Nixon denied any knowledge of or connection to this crime, a group of men employed at the White House was arrested and charged, while several Nixon staffers were found to have helped cover up the crime.

A former aide to Nixon testified that the president had secretly recorded conversations with his aides, and the tapes were subpoenaed as evidence in the investigation into the break-in. Nixon released only a portion of the tapes when forced to do so, and investigators found that parts of those tapes had been erased. Still, there was enough evidence for the House to take action. In July 1974, three articles of impeachment, including abuse of power and contempt of Congress, were recommended by the House Judiciary Committee. But before the House could vote on whether to impeach him, Nixon resigned on August 9, 1974.

President Bill Clinton's impeachment case was very different from that of Johnson or Nixon. From November 1995 to April 1996, Clinton had an affair with a White House intern, Monica Lewinsky. After Lewinsky left the White House in April 1996 to work in the Pentagon, she told coworker Linda Tripp about the affair, which had sporadically continued through 1997. Tripp secretly recorded several of these conversations with Lewinsky. Tripp took the recordings to Kenneth Starr, a lawyer who was investigating the real estate investments of Clinton and his wife, Hillary Clinton. Initially President Clinton lied about the affair, so when the House drew up the articles of impeachment, the charges were perjury, or lying under oath, and obstruction of justice. Like Johnson and Trump, Clinton was not convicted or removed from office, but all three have been impeached.

FROM THE HEADLINES

GUILT AND REMOVAL

Of the 20 impeached US officials, only eight have been found guilty and removed from office. All eight were judges.

John Pickering had been sick for several years before he was convicted on March 12, 1804. The charges included mishandling a trial, being intoxicated in court, and swearing in court. His conviction was controversial because he had committed no crime by law, though he was unfit to serve as a judge.

West Humphreys was convicted on June 26, 1862, because he supported secession when the Southern states split from the North during the Civil War. After secession, he served as a Confederate judge in Tennessee. In this position, he seized property of people who supported the North.

Robert Archbald was convicted January 13, 1913, for profiting from both coal mining and railroading due to his position. As a commerce judge, he often heard cases involving these two industries. He unethically used the inside knowledge he gained to invest and recommend land for purchase.

Halsted Ritter was convicted on April 17, 1936. He had appointed someone to a position for a $4,500 kickback. He then lied on his taxes, committing tax evasion.

Harry Claiborne was impeached on October 9, 1986. He had been convicted in criminal court in 1984 for lying on his tax returns. The criminal conviction put him in jail, but he still received his salary. The only way to quit paying him was to impeach him to remove him from his job.

Alcee Hastings was impeached on October 20, 1989, for accepting a bribe to reduce a sentence. He had been charged and acquitted for this crime in criminal court, but the impeachment charges included perjury and tampering with evidence, both proved in the Senate hearing.

Walter Nixon was convicted on November 3, 1989, for perjury while he was being investigated for bribery. He refused to resign in jail, so he was impeached.

Thomas Porteous was convicted on December 8, 2010, for bribery and corruption.

Judge Thomas Porteous was removed from office after being impeached and convicted of bribery and corruption in 2010.

CHAPTER THREE

THREATS AND
INVESTIGATIONS

In September 2015, the Federal Bureau of Investigation (FBI) contacted the DNC because Russian hackers had found a way into the DNC's computer system. But the DNC failed to find its own evidence, so it ignored the warning. The FBI contacted the DNC again in November to say at least one of the DNC's computers was transmitting data to a computer in Russia. Despite attempts to block these infiltrations, by June 2016, Russian hackers had stolen thousands of emails from the DNC's server. Later investigation showed that hackers working for the Russian government were determined to meddle in the US political process.

Meanwhile, the US Department of State, also known as the State Department, had been investigating Hillary

The DNC headquarters is in Washington, DC.

Clinton's use of a private email server while she was secretary of state during President Barack Obama's first term. At the time of this investigation, Clinton was running for president—an election that she would eventually lose to Trump. Investigators found that some of Clinton's emails from the private server had been deleted. This raised concerns about the content of the deleted messages.

In May 2016, the State Department said Clinton's use of this private email account was inappropriate. It was not criminal, but she would not have received permission to use the private server if she had asked. On July 5, 2016, FBI director James Comey said an investigation had shown Clinton may have mishandled confidential information but that there was not enough evidence for prosecution.

During a press conference on July 27, 2016, Trump discussed his rival Clinton's use of this server. He called on hackers to find the deleted messages. "Russia, if you're listening, I hope you're able to find the 30,000 emails that are missing," Trump said.[1] Trump's supporters, including former house speaker Newt Gingrich, a Republican, said Trump was only joking. But Trump's critics had doubts. "This has to be the first time that a major presidential

Comey testifies before the House Oversight Committee in July 2016 to explain the FBI's recommendation to not prosecute Clinton.

candidate has actively encouraged a foreign power to conduct espionage against his political opponent," said Jake Sullivan, an adviser for Hillary Clinton's campaign.[2]

Concern about Russian hackers rose on August 12, 2016, when hackers published the private cell phone numbers and email addresses of House Speaker Nancy Pelosi and other high-ranking Democrats. Federal investigations into these hacking attacks continued. On October 7, 2016, the Department of Homeland Security stated that the intelligence community was certain the Russian government was behind the hacks.

Trump celebrates with his family during his election night victory rally.

PRESIDENT TRUMP

When Trump, a Republican, won the presidential election on November 8, 2016, it was an upset. Hillary Clinton, a Democrat, won the popular vote, taking 65.8 million votes to Trump's 62.9 million. But winning the presidency relies on the electoral college, not the popular vote. In the electoral college, each state controls a specific number of electoral votes. The presidential election is decided by the number of electoral votes a candidate receives. Trump needed 270 electoral votes to win, and he received 304 electoral votes to Clinton's 227.[3]

News reports in November and December on the ongoing findings of the intelligence community said there was evidence that the hackers, or whoever hired them, intended to interfere with the election. The report did not say Trump had benefited from the interference. Still, Clinton supporters were suspicious because only the DNC and Clinton campaigners were affected.

By the time Trump was sworn in as president on January 20, 2017, the FBI was investigating the Russian interference. On January 6, 2017, the director of national intelligence had released a report detailing how Russian president Vladimir Putin had led an effort to interfere in the US presidential election to help Trump by damaging Clinton's reputation.

On March 2, 2017, the head of the Justice Department, then attorney general Jeff Sessions, recused himself from investigating whether Trump's campaign had conspired with the Russians. A Justice Department rule states no one in the department can investigate someone with whom they have a personal or political relationship. Sessions was an adviser for Trump's presidential campaign.

FBI FIRING

The FBI continued to investigate, looking for evidence that Trump had encouraged the interference or accepted support from the hackers. Then on May 9, 2017, President Trump fired Comey. Trump said the firing had been recommended by Justice Department officials, including Sessions. Two days later, Trump was interviewed by NBC *Nightly News* anchor Lester Holt. The president called Comey incompetent. Trump also admitted to Holt that he was thinking about the Russia investigation when he fired Comey. "Regardless of the recommendation, I was going to fire Comey knowing there was no good time to do it," Trump said.[4]

Comey's firing led to the first article of impeachment filed against the president. In July 2017, House Democrats Brad Sherman of California and Al Green of Texas filed an article accusing Trump of obstructing justice, both by firing Comey to undermine the FBI's investigation and by attempting to thwart an investigation of national security adviser Michael Flynn. This recommendation by Sherman and Green went nowhere because the Republicans in the House majority sided with the president. Many Democrats did not support this impeachment attempt either, partly due to concerns about how it could affect upcoming elections.

After he was fired by Trump, Comey and the FBI were investigated by the Justice Department to review the FBI's investigation into Hillary Clinton's emails. Inspector General Michael Horowitz did not find a pro-Clinton bias within the FBI, but he did find that the FBI's investigation failed to follow proper procedures. Horowitz then looked into FBI procedures used when seeking permission to monitor someone's electronic communications. In this latter investigation, Horowitz found problems in every application used for monitoring that his department reviewed. These problems ranged from typos to misreported facts and

MICHAEL FLYNN

After winning the election, Trump selected retired US Army lieutenant general Michael Flynn as his national security adviser. Before Trump's inauguration, Flynn told a Russian official that the incoming Trump administration would be friendlier to Russia than the outgoing Obama administration, which had imposed sanctions on Russia for its election interference. The FBI interviewed Flynn about these calls, and he said he had not discussed the sanctions. The FBI, which had been monitoring the Russian official's communications, knew Flynn was lying. He was then charged with lying to the FBI, which is a crime. In May 2020, the Justice Department announced it planned to have the judge dismiss the case. The department said there had been no active investigation into Flynn, so even though he had lied, it wasn't a crime. Flynn's lawyers also said the FBI had intentionally tried to get him to lie, a situation called entrapment. At the same time, some legal experts argued that the FBI had treated Flynn the same as other interviewees. The judge in the case decided not to dismiss it right away, instead appointing a former federal judge to assess the request. The former judge argued that the request to drop the case was political in nature, rather than being based in fact. In June, a federal appeals court ordered the judge to dismiss the case, though future appeals were possible.

missing documentation. In response to these findings, an FBI official told a reporter that FBI procedures were being changed to prevent future errors.

THE MUELLER REPORT

Investigations into the Russian hacking did not stop with Comey's dismissal. On May 17, 2017, Deputy Attorney General Rod Rosenstein appointed former FBI director Robert Mueller as special counsel, a lawyer assigned to a specific task. Mueller's job was to investigate the Russian government's efforts to influence the US election and connection to Trump's campaign.

Mueller's investigation took nearly two years. While it was underway, Americans in some states voted for US representatives and senators in November 2018. The Democrats won enough seats in the House to have the majority. Talk of impeachment resumed, and Sherman and Green immediately reintroduced their articles of impeachment. House Speaker Nancy Pelosi urged Democrats to wait until Mueller finished his investigation.

During the investigation, some people who had worked with Trump's campaign were arrested and criminally charged, though the charges were not directly connected to the Russian interference. These included Paul Manafort, Trump's former campaign chairman; Michael Cohen, Trump's former personal lawyer; and George Papadopoulos, a former Trump campaign adviser. Manafort and Cohen were found guilty of financial crimes. Papadopoulos was found guilty of lying to FBI investigators about Russian contacts.

Once Mueller's investigation was complete, he sent his final report to the Justice Department before delivering it to Congress. On April 18, 2019, Attorney General William Barr held a press conference where he praised Trump for providing access to the documents Mueller needed in the investigation. Barr stated that, in short, there was no collusion. Reporters had not seen the report, and Barr left the press conference before they could ask questions.

Later that day, Mueller delivered to Congress what has come to be known as the Mueller Report. The report confirmed that there was no clear evidence Trump or his campaign colluded with Russia to affect the 2016 election. The document did detail how people associated with Trump had obstructed the investigation by lying to investigators. In addition, Mueller reported that Trump refused to answer any questions about whether he had encouraged people to lie to investigators. In the report, Mueller discussed what he called social media warfare, which includes foreign entities purchasing and running political ads. Mueller also reported how Russian hackers had accessed state databases to get information on millions of voters. Mueller detailed meetings that Trump's associates, including his son Donald Trump Jr. and his son-in-law, Jared Kushner, had with representatives from Russia. The report also condemned Trump for demanding that Sessions reverse his decision to recuse himself.

In line with the Justice Department policy that a sitting president cannot be indicted or criminally charged, the Mueller report did not call for a criminal trial or say Trump was innocent. The report noted that there is a constitutional process for addressing presidential misconduct. That process is impeachment.

MORE TO THE
STORY

CHRISTOPHER STEELE

In April 2016, the DNC and the Clinton campaign hired research company Fusion GPS to investigate Trump. In June, Fusion GPS hired Russia expert and former British spy Christopher Steele to look into any potential connections between Trump and Russia. Steele's findings, obtained using sources in Russia, alarmed him, and he sent this information to the FBI. His sources suggested that Russia favored Trump, that the Trump campaign was accepting help from Russia, and that Russia had compromising information that it could use to blackmail Trump. The FBI felt that Steele's background made him credible. Steele's information was key in the FBI obtaining a surveillance order for Trump campaign aide Carter Page, who had ties to Russia.

However, the US Department of Justice's Office of the Inspector General found issues with the FBI's work. In a report released in December 2019, it said the FBI did not verify the information Steele provided and that it had omitted key details in seeking the surveillance order. Some footnotes in the report were redacted, or blacked out. In April 2020, some of those footnotes were released publicly. These footnotes say that the FBI had received warnings that the Russian government may have intentionally provided false information to Steele. The Steele information played little role in the Mueller Report. But to some, the saga was evidence of how the FBI's investigation into Trump was flawed. In a statement released in April 2020, Republican senators Chuck Grassley and Ron Johnson said, "As we can see from these now-declassified footnotes in the IG's report . . . the FBI had reports in hand that their central piece of evidence was most likely tainted with Russian disinformation."[6]

CHAPTER FOUR

IMPEACHMENT
INQUIRY

O n September 20, 2019, the *Wall Street Journal* published an article about a July 25, 2019, phone call President Trump made to the new Ukrainian president, Volodymyr Zelensky. A whistleblower, or an anonymous witness, had come forward and revealed details of the call. In the conversation, Trump pushed Zelensky to work with lawyer Rudy Giuliani to investigate Hunter Biden, the son of Trump's political opponent Joe Biden.

In April 2014, Hunter Biden had become a board member for the Burisma Group, a Ukrainian energy exploration company. At that time, his father, Joe Biden, was vice president of the United States under President Barack Obama. The vice president's job included working

Volodymyr Zelensky became president of Ukraine in 2019.

with Ukrainian politicians, and Joe Biden encouraged them to work against corruption in their country. Work against corruption led to an investigation of Burisma by Ukrainian general prosecutor Viktor Shokin, who was eventually fired. On May 16, 2019, Ukrainian officials said this investigation found no wrongdoing by either Biden.

WHISTLEBLOWERS

A whistleblower is anyone who sees something illegal, unethical, or dangerous in business or government and reveals this to authorities or the public. In England in the late 1500s, "to whistle" meant to expose a secret. By the early twentieth century, people were called whistleblowers whenever they protested something immoral or illegal in the hopes of bringing it to a halt.

In the *Wall Street Journal* article, the anonymous source did not believe that Trump mentioned potential monetary aid to Ukraine, although the concept of quid pro quo would later become an issue. Quid pro quo refers to a favor that one person expects in return for doing something for someone else. In this case, it would later become a question of whether President Trump told President Zelensky that, if Ukraine announced an investigation into Hunter Biden and Burisma, the United States would release almost $400 million in promised military aid to Ukraine.

INQUIRY ANNOUNCED

After the article was published, Trump admitted that he had discussed Hunter Biden with Zelensky, but he said that he did not pressure the Ukrainian president to investigate Biden. According to Trump, the point of the phone call had been to congratulate Zelensky on winning the election. When asked about withheld military aid, Trump again denied connecting this aid to Biden or coercing Zelensky to relaunch the investigation. Instead, Trump said that aid had been withheld in an attempt to get European nations to step forward and aid Ukraine instead of expecting money to come from the United States.

Only later did the full timeline of the aid become clear. By July 18, the aid had been held. The call with Zelensky was one week later, on July 25. The American press learned of the hold by August 28, when the website Politico published an article about it. House investigations into Trump's alleged pressuring of Ukraine began on September 9, and the aid was released on September 11.

Trump's phone call with Zelensky had not been recorded, but notes had been taken throughout. When

Hunter Biden, *right*, attends a college basketball game with his father in 2010.

the notes on the phone call were made public, people could see what had been discussed. "Congratulations on a great victory. We all watched from the United States, and you did a terrific job. The way you came from behind, somebody who wasn't given much of a chance, and you ended up winning easily. It's a fantastic achievement. Congratulations," Trump said in the call notes.[1] Trump did, as he claimed, congratulate Zelensky on winning the election.

But Trump also brought up investigating possible interference in US elections. Trump mentioned Mueller's report, which detailed investigations into election interference, but then Trump pointed to Ukraine as the

44

source of the problem. US intelligence officials already knew that Russian hackers were responsible, but a rumor had been spread by Russian sources that Ukrainians were behind it all. Zelensky assured Trump that Ukraine wanted to cooperate with the United States to secure good relations between the two countries.

It was after this that Trump brought up the Bidens. As President Obama's vice president from 2009 to 2017, Joe Biden had advised Ukrainian leaders that international aid to stand against Russia would only come if they rid Ukraine of corruption throughout its government and government-owned energy companies. Burisma, in contrast, was small and privately owned. In 2014, when Joe Biden's US political opponents questioned Hunter Biden's position on the Burisma board, a State Department spokesperson said the US government was not concerned about a conflict of interest. The call notes say Trump told Zelensky that anything the Ukrainian president could do to work with the US attorney general to investigate the Bidens would be appreciated.

According to the call notes, Zelensky responded positively, saying that Trump's request would be feasible.

FROM THE
HEADLINES

UKRAINE

From 1922 to 1991, the Soviet Union stretched across Europe and Asia. When this confederation of communist countries dissolved, new alliances were formed. Russia competed for allies against Western Europe and the United States. Ukraine, one of the countries of the former Soviet Union, was a powerhouse because it was the location of approximately 1,800 nuclear warheads, 176 long-range ballistic missiles, and 42 bombers.[2] The newly independent nation also had the uranium deposits and technical knowledge to build more. It remained allied with Russia until 2014, when a revolution removed Ukraine's corrupt president, Viktor Yanukovych, from office. Because Yanukovych was a Russian ally, Russia responded by invading and seizing Ukraine's Crimea peninsula and is still fighting in Ukraine today.

Russia has a history of taking an active role in the affairs of neighboring countries that were once part of the Soviet Union, including Ukraine.

He said, "Since we have won the absolute majority in our Parliament, the next prosecutor general will be 100 percent my person, my candidate, who will be approved, by the parliament and will start as a new prosecutor in September. He or she will look into the situation, specifically to the company that you mentioned in this issue."[3]

When the Democrats took the majority of seats in the House in January 2019, Pelosi and other prominent Democrats had spoken against demands for presidential impeachment. They felt that moderate Democrats would have a harder time getting reelected in 2020 if the party tried to impeach the president. But the news about Trump's discussions with Zelensky changed this. After news of the phone call came out, House Democrats strongly supported an impeachment inquiry, which is an information-gathering step that precedes impeachment and a Senate trial. It was during one of these information-gathering meetings that Laura Cooper

MORE TO THE
STORY

PUBLIC REACTION

Americans offered a mix of responses to BBC reporters when asked how they felt about the allegations against Trump and the impeachment inquiry. One woman said about the Democratic House, "Run the government. Do what you're supposed to do. Don't go after a man you shouldn't be going after. He's our president and now work together."[5] But others supported the impeachment process, including one woman who said, "I think they should impeach him. . . . He's violated so many clauses of the Constitution that they need to pursue it."[6] Regardless of whether the impeachment inquiry would lead to Trump being removed from office, some people believed a message needed to be sent. "They have to at least impeach him, even if it'll come to nothing, just to show the American people that they understand that crimes have been committed," said one man.[7] When a National Public Radio call-in show talked with people across the United States, one man said, "I think that the president just needs to do his job. People need to let him do it. It's too much nitpicking and trying to impeach him. It's just ridiculous. If someone was on my shoulders all day, I wouldn't be able to do my job . . . or looking over my shoulder or beating me down every chance they get."[8]

was set to give her deposition and Republicans protested by forcing their way into the SCIF.

THE HOUSE PROCEEDS

In starting with an inquiry, the House was proceeding differently than it had when President Bill Clinton was impeached. That time, the House of Representatives voted to hold hearings to study whether Clinton should be investigated. In the case of President Trump, no such resolution was introduced or passed, but the Constitution does not say that a vote has to take place. Because of this, such a vote is a precedent—following the practice that has taken place in the past—but it is not legally required. With President Trump, individual committees started investigating what fell within their jurisdictions. When these committees had finished taking depositions and gathering the information, it was all presented to the House Judiciary Committee.

It was then the Judiciary Committee's job to read through all the information and recommend specific impeachment charges or articles of impeachment. Most of the committee's members approved of two impeachment articles—abuse of power and obstruction of Congress, or preventing Congress from doing its job. The articles said that Trump abused his power by asking Ukraine to take actions that would affect the 2020 presidential election in a way that would benefit him personally. This alleged abuse of power was also against the interests of the United States by compromising the nation's security and undermining the US election process. And Trump allegedly obstructed Congress by refusing to recognize the House as the sole authority to impeach an official. Trump had reportedly instructed members of his administration to ignore the House's requests for information, putting himself above Congress in the matter of his own possible impeachment. Once the Judiciary Committee delivered these articles to the full House, it was time for an open, public investigation.

CHAPTER FIVE

PUBLIC
HEARINGS

O n October 28, 2019, Nancy Pelosi wrote a letter to Democratic members of Congress stating that the House would begin formal impeachment proceedings against President Trump. "We are taking this step to eliminate any doubt as to whether the Trump administration may withhold documents, prevent witness testimony, disregard duly authorized subpoenas, or continue obstructing the House of Representatives," Pelosi said in the letter, which was released to the public.[1]

Up until this point, the White House, under President Trump's direction, had refused to comply with requests from the various House committees asking for information, records, or interviews.

Pelosi speaks to reporters about the House's impeachment investigation of Trump.

White House officials said the reason for their lack of cooperation was that they believed the procedure was not legitimate because the House had not voted on whether to investigate the president. The White House quickly responded to Pelosi's letter. "We won't be able to comment fully until we see the actual text, but Speaker Pelosi is finally admitting what the rest of America already knew—that Democrats were conducting an unauthorized impeachment proceeding, refusing to give the President due process, and their secret, shady, closed door depositions are completely and irreversibly illegitimate," said White House Press Secretary Stephanie Grisham.[2]

The next steps included a vote in the House followed by public hearings. At this time, Trump and his lawyers would be invited to take part. Once the public hearings were

REPUBLICAN DISAPPROVAL

Critical Republican responses to Pelosi's announcement of an impeachment inquiry came from more than just the White House. House Minority Leader Kevin McCarthy, a Republican representing California, tweeted his displeasure, stating in part, "This process has been botched from the start. We will not legitimize the Schiff/Pelosi sham impeachment."[3] Representative Greg Walden of Oregon spoke to reporters. "It's been a bad process . . . and this is a very, very serious matter—when you're talking about impeaching the president of the United States, you better do it right. And so far, I don't think they have," he said.[4]

completed, the House Judiciary Committee would review all materials gathered.

INTELLIGENCE COMMITTEE HEARINGS

The Intelligence Committee held the first public impeachment hearings on November 13, 2019. The committee called high-profile witnesses to testify. These included Lieutenant Colonel Alexander Vindman, a National Security Council expert on Ukraine; Jennifer Williams, an aide to Vice President Mike Pence; Lieutenant General Keith Kellogg, a member of Pence's staff; Fiona Hill, a former member of the National Security Council; and Gordon Sondland, the US ambassador to the European Union.

Vindman had been present when President Trump telephoned Zelensky. Vindman testified that he couldn't believe it when, during the conversation, he heard Trump mention investigations into the Bidens and an unproven theory that Ukrainian hackers had interfered with the 2016

"THE AMERICAN PEOPLE WILL HEAR FIRSTHAND ABOUT THE PRESIDENT'S MISCONDUCT."[5]

—HOUSE INTELLIGENCE COMMITTEE CHAIR ADAM SCHIFF, 2019

presidential elections. "It is improper for the president of the United States to demand a foreign government investigate a US citizen and political opponent," Vindman said.[6] He was so disturbed by what he heard that he had reported it to the National Security Council's top lawyer.

Williams, a national security aide to Pence, agreed with Vindman. She testified that the president's call with Zelensky was very unusual because he mentioned a domestic political matter when he brought up Biden. When Williams's supervisor, Kellogg, testified, he disagreed. He said he heard nothing inappropriate. Kellogg added that Williams had not come to him with any concerns at the time of the call, something that he said should have happened if she believed Trump had behaved inappropriately.

Other witnesses provided evidence that the White House had been pushing for an investigation of the Bidens. On July 10, before the call, Ukrainian and US officials met at the White House. Hill, an expert on Russia, was there. She testified that as the meeting was ending, the Ukrainians asked when Trump would meet with Zelensky. Hill's supervisor tried to change the subject, but then, Hill said, "Ambassador Sondland leaned in basically to say, well, well we have an agreement that there will be a meeting if specific investigations are put underway."[7] At the time, Hill said, she believed the White House's push for a new investigation was going to cause trouble. "And here we are," she said during her testimony.[8]

Sondland also testified about the push for an investigation. He said that not only had Giuliani requested an investigation but that it had been a quid pro quo request. "Mr. Giuliani's requests were a quid pro quo, arranging a White House visit for President Zelensky. Mr. Giuliani demanded that Ukraine make a public statement announcing the investigations of the 2016 election DNC server and Burisma," Sondland said.[9]

SONDLAND'S DONATION

Like many ambassadors, Sondland owed his position directly to the president, as the president nominates ambassadors. Sondland, whose background is in hotel ownership, had limited political experience before getting the post as the US ambassador to the European Union. He got the job after he donated $1 million to Trump's inauguration committee.

JUDICIARY COMMITTEE HEARINGS

For two weeks the House Intelligence Committee held hearings to gather evidence concerning possible inappropriate behavior by the president. Only then did the House Judiciary Committee take over under the leadership of Representative Jerry Nadler, a Democrat from New York. On December 4, 2019, this committee began taking testimony from four constitutional law scholars: Noah Feldman of Harvard University in Cambridge, Massachusetts; Pamela Karlan of Stanford University in Stanford, California; Michael Gerhardt of the University of North Carolina at Chapel Hill; and Jonathan Turley of George Washington University in Washington, DC.

Feldman, Karlan, and Gerhardt were chosen by the Democrats on the committee, while the Republicans chose Turley. The Democrats' three experts recommended impeachment. "If left unchecked, the president will likely continue his pattern of soliciting foreign interference on his behalf in the next election," Gerhardt said.[10]

Several Republican representatives challenged these three scholars, saying they had come to the hearing already biased against Trump. Matt Gaetz, a Republican representing Florida, pointed out that Gerhardt had contributed to Obama's presidential campaign and Karlan donated to the campaigns of Obama, Hillary Clinton, and

Senator Elizabeth Warren. Tom McClintock, a Republican representing California, demanded that the witnesses raise their hands if they voted for Trump, but they refused to do so. "I have the right to a secret ballot," Karlan said.[11]

The Republican's choice, Turley, argued that the case for impeachment was careless and premature. He said a quid pro quo for an investigation against a rival in exchange for military aid would be an impeachable offense, but only if it had been proven with hard evidence. He predicted that without stronger evidence, the case against Trump would not make it through a Senate trial.

The House Judiciary Committee had 41 members during the Trump impeachment inquiry.

The Judiciary Committee invited President Trump and his lawyers to attend these hearings, but the invitation was declined. White House counsel Pat Cipollone said that neither President Trump nor his lawyers would be present because the hearing did not have a clear-cut purpose and because they believed the impeachment inquiry procedures so far had already been problematic.

In the end, the Judiciary Committee produced a 658-page report detailing the impeachment inquiry. It included two articles of impeachment, one for abuse of power and the other for obstructing Congress. The committee said the situation with Ukraine was not the first time the president had sought foreign interference to influence a US election and, unless he was stopped, it would not be the last.

The Republicans on the committee openly criticized the report and its findings. Representative Doug Collins

"IF THE HOUSE PROCEEDS SOLELY ON THE UKRAINIAN ALLEGATIONS, THIS IMPEACHMENT WOULD STAND OUT AMONG MODERN IMPEACHMENTS AS THE SHORTEST PROCEEDING, WITH THE THINNEST EVIDENTIARY RECORD, AND THE NARROWEST GROUNDS EVER USED TO IMPEACH A PRESIDENT."[12]

—JONATHAN TURLEY, CONSTITUTIONAL LAW EXPERT, 2019

of Georgia said that no impeachable offense had been proven. "An accusation of abuse of power must be based on a higher and more concrete standard than conduct that 'ignored and injured the interests of the Nation,'" Collins said, quoting the committee report.[13] But this was not the majority opinion of the Judiciary Committee, so the impeachment process moved forward.

THE REPUBLICAN REPORT

Before the official Intelligence Committee Report was released to the Judiciary Committee, Republican members of the Intelligence Committee had already released their own report. It stated that because the American people elected President Trump, this impeachment inquiry was an attempt to reverse the will of the people and an attempt to stop the president from being reelected. In addition, they said that the inquiry was not the result of presidential misconduct but part of a campaign to overthrow the US political process. About Ukraine, the report said that the inquiry ignored Ukrainian strides against corruption and that it was Ukraine, not Russia, that interfered in the 2016 presidential election.

ARTICLES OF
IMPEACHMENT

O n December 5, 2019, Pelosi entered the chamber
of the House of Representatives. She reminded
the gathered representatives that when the
Constitution was drafted, James Madison, who wrote
much of that document, included provisions to keep
the United States from falling under the rule of a tyrant
like King George III, who reigned when the states were
British colonies. Pelosi explained, "The founders feared
the return of a monarchy in America. And having just
fought a war of independence, they specifically feared
the prospect of a king-president corrupted by foreign
influence."[1]

Pelosi concluded her statement by asking the
chairman of the Judiciary Committee, Representative

Pelosi, *left*, and House Judiciary Committee Chairman Jerry Nadler, *right*,
lead a group of representatives to publicly announce the articles of
impeachment against Trump.

Jerry Nadler, to move forward in preparing the articles of impeachment. Pelosi explained that creating the articles of impeachment was necessary because Trump had used the office of president to ask a foreign power to interfere in the US political process for his own benefit. These articles would specify the charges against the president and why each charge had been chosen.

BACK TO COMMITTEE

The Judiciary Committee spent three days discussing the articles of impeachment. They eventually settled on two articles. Article I was for abuse of power, and Article II was for obstruction of Congress. The third day's discussion, on December 12, was 14 hours long, largely because of numerous amendments, or changes and additions, proposed by Republican representatives on the committee.

The first of these amendments was proposed by Jim Jordan, a Republican representing Ohio, at 9:32 a.m. "This amendment strikes Article I because Article I ignores the truth," Jordan said.[2] According to Jordan, there had been no abuse of power because the evidence found in the course of the investigation was untrue. He said that if the president had withheld Ukrainian aid for political reasons, representatives of Ukraine could have objected through phone calls or meetings. The debate on this first amendment lasted for three hours and failed with the Republicans voting for the amendment and the Democrats voting against it. Throughout the day, arguments continued to fall along party lines.

"I THINK LEADERSHIP WANTS ALL OF US TO DO BEST FOR OUR DISTRICT AND MAKE A DECISION BASED ON THE FACTS."[4]

—REPRESENTATIVE JOSH GOTTHEIMER, DEMOCRAT OF NEW JERSEY, SPEAKING ON THE IMPEACHMENT PROCESS, 2019

The next amendment was proposed by Matt Gaetz, a Republican representing Florida, who wanted to insert phrasing about what he said was well-known corruption surrounding Burisma and its hiring of Hunter Biden. "It's a little hard to believe that Burisma hired Hunter Biden to resolve their international disputes when he could not resolve his own dispute with Hertz Rental Car over leaving cocaine in a crack pipe in the car," he said.[3] This comment referred to a 2016 incident in which drugs were found in a car Hunter Biden had used but for which he was never criminally charged. Hank Johnson, a Democrat representing Georgia, called Gaetz's comment hypocritical, noting that Gaetz was arrested for but not convicted of driving under the influence in 2008. This amendment was voted down 23 to 17.[5]

Additional amendments were proposed. One requested adding language saying that the Ukrainian aid was eventually released. Another was to strike the second article. A third proposed striking the last eight lines of text from both articles. This paragraph, found at the end of each article, states that Trump has shown he will continue to be a threat to the Constitution unless impeached and should not be allowed to hold any other office. All proposed amendments failed, and this phase ended at 11:16 p.m.

The Judiciary Committee could have voted on the articles of impeachment, but Nadler

DRUG CHARGES AGAINST HUNTER BIDEN

In 2019, Hunter Biden spoke to the *New Yorker* magazine about drug addiction. He knew that with his father's presidential campaign, bits and pieces of the story would come out, and he wanted to get ahead of that. He said he first abused alcohol in high school. Then in college, he started smoking cigarettes and using cocaine. A positive test for cocaine led to his discharge from the US Navy. He returned a rental car in Arizona in 2016 with a crack pipe and cocaine residue in the back, but he was never charged because there was no evidence he had used the pipe. As is true for many recovering addicts, Biden said his struggles were ongoing. "You don't get rid of it," he said. "You figure out how to deal with it."[6]

postponed the vote until the next morning. Republicans criticized this move because, as Doug Collins of Georgia said, they had not been consulted. A member of the committee's staff told CBS News that the decision had been made because of frequent Republican complaints about transparency. So, instead of voting in the dark of night, Nadler chose to schedule the vote for the following day. At ten the next morning, the committee voted for the articles one at a time. Both passed, and they were then sent on to the full House of Representatives.

DEBATE

Once the articles made it to the full House on December 18, 2019, there were another eight hours of debate. Although it is called debate, this was not a discussion between the Democrats and the Republicans with each side speaking to and listening to the other. Similarly to what had happened in the House Judiciary Committee debate, Democrats spoke to condemn Trump's actions while Republicans made a variety of motions, appeals, and rejections. To outsiders, it may have looked like the Republicans were wasting time, but

Representative Matt Gaetz was among the members of Congress who focused attention on controversies surrounding Hunter Biden.

this is a time-honored tradition for whichever party is in the minority. Party members' actions and words serve as symbols that they object to what is happening, even if they cannot stop it.

That evening, the House of Representatives voted on the articles of impeachment. Article I, on the abuse of power, passed with 230 representatives voting for it, 197 voting against, and one voting present. Article II, on obstructing Congress, passed with 229 representatives voting for it, 198 voting against it, and one voting present.[7]

For the most part, representatives voted along party lines, but there were a few exceptions. The lone

Independent, Justin Amash, representing Michigan, voted for both articles. Two Democrats did not vote with the rest of their party. Collin Peterson, representing Minnesota, voted against the articles of impeachment, while Tulsi Gabbard, representing Hawaii, voted present on both articles. By voting present, Gabbard refused to take sides but was counted for the quorum, the minimum number of representatives required for a vote to be legal. Gabbard explained her decision. "I am standing in the center and have decided to vote present. I could not in good conscience vote

VOTING SEPARATELY

When the time comes to vote on articles of impeachment in the House or Senate, each article is voted on separately. This is because each article is a separate charge, and some representatives or senators may think the president is guilty of one charge but not the other. Because of this, some might vote for one and against the other.

against impeachment because I believe President Trump is guilty of wrongdoing," Gabbard said. "I also could not in good conscience vote for impeachment because removal of a sitting president must not be the culmination of a partisan process, fueled by tribal animosities that have so gravely divided our country."[8] Still, with Democrats holding the House majority, the articles of impeachment passed, and the House moved on to the next step.

After passing the articles, a delay of approximately three weeks occurred in the impeachment process. Pelosi and other top Democrats used this time to negotiate with Senate Majority Leader Mitch McConnell, a Republican, asking him to agree to allow the Senate to call witnesses during the forthcoming public impeachment trial. Among witnesses the Democrats wanted to call was John Bolton, a former member of the National Security Council who declined to testify in the House but later agreed to testify before the Senate if asked. The Democrats knew the impeachment trial was very unlikely to result in a conviction because the Republicans were the majority in the Senate. Still, Democratic leaders decided to see the process through.

TWO TEAMS

The last step for the House of Representatives was for Pelosi to name the House managers. These managers would act as prosecutors in the Senate trial. In their first official duty, they would deliver the articles of impeachment to the Senate.

The seven Democrats Pelosi chose on January 15, 2020, differed in age and background. Her goal was to reflect the full diversity of the American people represented by the Democratic Party. Retired army ranger Jason Crow, a Democrat representing Colorado, didn't serve on any of the House committees involved in the impeachment but was selected because he understood the importance of the military aid temporarily withheld by Trump. Val Demings, a Democrat representing Florida, went to segregated schools as a child and was the first female police chief in Orlando, Florida. Nadler, Schiff, and Hakeem Jeffries, a Democrat representing New York, were all lawyers. Sylvia Garcia, a Democrat representing Texas, was a lawyer and also served as a judge. And Zoe Lofgren, a Democrat representing California, also a lawyer, had been a Judiciary Committee staff member

"WE KNOW HOW IT'S GOING TO END. THERE IS NO CHANCE THE PRESIDENT IS GOING TO BE REMOVED FROM OFFICE."[9]

—SENATE MAJORITY LEADER MITCH MCCONNELL, 2019

during Nixon's impeachment inquiry and served on the committee during Clinton's impeachment.

Meanwhile, Trump gathered a team of lawyers to defend him during the Senate trial. Among them was Ken Starr, who worked to impeach President Bill Clinton. But the lawyers on his team were selected for more than their knowledge of the law. Trump understood that his team would be defending him not only in the Senate but also with the American voters. Because of this, according to a source who knows the president well and spoke to CNN, the president also selected people with big personalities. He knew that his spokespeople had to be able to defend him through the media to win over the American people, especially now that an impeachment trial was upon him.

MORE TO THE
STORY

KEN STARR

Working as an independent counsel, Ken Starr investigated Hillary and Bill Clinton's real estate investments in the 1990s. Later he investigated Bill Clinton's relationship with Monica Lewinsky. Based on Starr's findings in the latter investigation, Clinton was impeached but not convicted by the Senate. Although Starr continued to investigate Clinton until 2002, no criminal charges were filed.

In 2010, Starr became the president of Baylor University in Waco, Texas. He was named the university's chancellor in 2013. While he held these positions, the university came under criticism for how it handled reports of sexual assault, some of which were alleged to have been committed by football players. Starr was forced to resign from the university, two years before he was hired as Trump's lawyer.

While defending Trump, one of Starr's arguments against the impeachment was that he noted how divisive the impeachment of Clinton had been. "It's filled with acrimony, and it divides the country like nothing else," Starr said.[10] He also discussed how, unlike with past attempts to impeach presidents, there were no specific crimes alleged in the effort to impeach Trump.

CHAPTER SEVEN

PREPARING
FOR TRIAL

O n January 15, 2020, Cheryl Johnson, clerk of the House of Representatives, carried the articles of impeachment from the House Chamber to the Senate. A pathway had been roped off so that the House managers could follow her through the Capitol Building as crowds of reporters snapped photos. When the group arrived at the Senate floor, Johnson made a formal announcement: she informed the Senate that the House had selected managers for the impeachment trial of President Donald Trump. Then she handed the articles over to Laura Dove, the Senate secretary for the majority. With this delivery, the impeachment moved from the House to the Senate, where preparations for the trial would begin.

House clerk Cheryl Johnson, *front left*, delivers the articles of impeachment to the Senate, accompanied by the House managers and another House staff member.

The US Senate Manual contains a detailed list of rules to be followed throughout an impeachment trial. The rules are based on the 26 rules originally adopted on March 2, 1868, for the trial of Andrew Johnson. These are not the only procedures that must be followed, because the Senate's role in impeachment is also discussed in the Constitution. Normally the vice president presides over the Senate, which means that at the time of the Trump impeachment, Vice President Pence would have fulfilled this role. But the Constitution also states that if the president cannot perform his or her job, the vice president takes on the president's duties. This would create a conflict of interest for a vice president presiding over the impeachment hearing of a president. To avoid this, the Constitution states that in the impeachment of a president, the chief justice of the Supreme Court will preside over the Senate.

On January 16, 2020, Chief Justice John Roberts was sworn in to preside over the Senate trial of President Trump. Roberts didn't relinquish his Supreme Court duties, which include hearing cases and reviewing the actions of the executive and legislative branches to make sure they do not violate the Constitution. During the Senate trial, Roberts performed his regular duties in the morning and then presided over the Senate in the afternoon.

Roberts's first official task of the impeachment trial was the swearing in of the senators. Americans could watch the impeachment proceedings on C-SPAN, a network that shows many government hearings on TV and online. Those who tuned in to see Roberts swear in the senators probably noticed this was not a normal day in the Senate. During an impeachment, every senator is required to

Senator Chuck Grassley, *left*, swears in Chief Justice John Roberts as the presiding officer of Trump's impeachment trial.

attend. They must remain seated at their desks at all times, not walking the floor. They cannot have their phones, so there are no emails or live tweets sent. Finally, there is no talking allowed. Questions had to be submitted in writing to Roberts.

WRIT OF SUMMONS

The Senate began its work by issuing a writ of summons to President Trump. This legal document told President Trump and his legal team that there would be a trial. Because impeachment is such an important issue, the document was topped by the nation's seal. In the impeachment process, the recipient of this standard document is allowed to answer the charges. The Senate gives a specific date and time for the recipient's written response to be delivered to the Senate Chamber. This call for a reply is not something the recipient is allowed to debate, as the document states: "Hereof you are not to fail."[1]

After the writ of summons is issued, both sides summarize their arguments in written trial briefs. First the House managers prepare their brief, detailing the charges

and the evidence. Then the
person being impeached and
his or her lawyers respond in
their own written brief.

TRIAL BRIEFS

A trial brief is a written legal
argument that is especially
important in a complex case
like an impeachment. A brief
summarizes the facts, evidence,

THE OATH

Before he could preside over the
impeachment trial, Chief Justice
John Roberts had to be sworn
in. In the oath, Roberts was
asked whether he would "do
impartial justice according to the
Constitution and the laws." As
expected, he responded, "I do."
Roberts then administered this
same oath to all 100 senators,
who also responded, as a group, "I
do." With this oath, both the chief
justice and the senators promised
to set aside their preconceived
ideas about what had occurred
and listen to the evidence.[2]

and arguments that will be presented during the trial. On

January 18, the House managers submitted their 111-page

brief, officially called the Impeachment Trial Memorandum.

This document restated the importance of two things:

first, the importance of impeachment as a tool to hold the

president to the law, and second, the constitutional power

of Congress to impeach the president. It then detailed

the allegation that Trump pushed Ukraine to investigate

the Bidens in return for military aid, and the charge that

he obstructed Congress by initially refusing to answer

questions about possible impeachment. Next, it presented

details of allegations that he interfered in the investigations, posed a national security threat by manipulating Ukraine, and didn't get the desired result from the manipulation. None of the information was new, but now Trump's team of lawyers could see what the House investigation had found.

The response by Trump's team, submitted on January 20, was even longer, at 171 pages. This brief started by answering the specific charges laid out in the articles of impeachment, stating, among other things, that Trump had not obstructed Congress but had instead defended the powers of the separate branches of government, specifically those of the executive branch. Through the brief, Trump's team argued that limiting the president's power in the way this impeachment was trying to do would permit Congress to threaten any president with impeachment simply for acting as president. The brief also condemned the House Democrats for having "secret hearings in a basement bunker," most likely a reference to the SCIF. The brief stated that the "House Democrats' standard of conduct for a President would open virtually every presidential decision to partisan attack based on questioning a President's motives."[3] Having filed their trial briefs, both sides were ready to have their say in the Senate.

"THEY FAIL TO ALLEGE ANY CRIME OR VIOLATION OF LAW WHATSOEVER."[4]

—PRESIDENT TRUMP'S LEGAL TEAM ON THE ARTICLES OF IMPEACHMENT

Ken Starr, one of Trump's lawyers, arrives at the US Capitol for the impeachment trial.

CHAPTER EIGHT

TRIAL AND ACQUITTAL

T he Senate wrote its rules for impeachment more than 100 years ago. Trump's trial opened with a 12-hour debate to fine-tune these rules. A final vote on the rules occurred shortly before two in the morning on January 22, 2020.

A key point of debate among the rules was whether new witnesses and evidence would be allowed. Senate Minority Leader Chuck Schumer, a Democrat from New York, proposed that the Senate issue subpoenas for documents from the White House, State Department, Pentagon, and Office of Management and Budget related to Ukraine. Earlier in the impeachment process, these documents had been withheld by Trump's administration, which had also blocked key witnesses

As Senate minority leader, Chuck Schumer was a key figure for the Senate Democrats during Trump's impeachment process.

from appearing before the House. Schumer and other Democratic senators wanted to bring in these witnesses and documents to see whether the executive branch had managed to keep the House from accessing key evidence.

One potential witness named by Democrats was Bolton, the former national security adviser who had declined to testify in front of the House but said he would speak to the Senate. Nadler, acting as a House manager, told the senators they should bring Bolton before the Senate so the group could learn the true extent of the president's crimes. Failure to do so would signal their willingness to cover up potential misconduct by the president, he said.

While discussing bringing in witnesses, Democrats and Republicans continued to insult each other. Roberts spoke up. "It is appropriate at this point for me to admonish both the House managers and the president's counsel in equal terms to remember that they are addressing the world's greatest deliberative body," he said.[1] The Senate approved the final rules, which focused on how long each side would have to present arguments, without making a final decision concerning new testimony or evidence. Making a final decision on these points would be postponed until a later date.

THE PROCESS

Opening arguments in the Senate trial started on January 22, 2020, with the House managers speaking first. In addition to presenting the facts, Schiff reminded senators that the information in the Intelligence Committee report was gathered at personal risk to the careers of civil servants and foreign service officers who had spoken with House investigators in defiance of orders from the White House.

"TO BLAME THE HOUSE FOR NOT HAVING ALL THE WITNESSES AND DOCUMENTS WHEN IT WAS DONALD TRUMP WHO STOPPED THEM AND WITH THE SNAP OF HIS FINGER CAN HAVE THEM ALL IS THE ULTIMATE HYPOCRISY."[2]

—SENATE MINORITY LEADER CHUCK SCHUMER, 2020

Once Schiff had finished his presentation, the president's team summarized its defense. The Ukrainian phone call wasn't Trump demanding an investigation intended to damage a political opponent, his lawyers said. Instead, they said, it was the president working to clean up corruption, meaning the disagreement with the Democrats was a simple policy dispute and not a matter worthy of impeachment. The president's team also said that even if Trump had withheld aid until Zelensky promised to investigate Hunter Biden, this would not be an impeachable offense. They also argued against calling witnesses.

After these opening arguments, senators had the opportunity to ask questions. All 180 questions were written out and given to Roberts. "The President's counsel argues that there was no harm done, that the aid was ultimately released to Ukraine . . . and that this President has treated Ukraine more favorably than his predecessors. What is your response?" asked Senator Patrick Leahy,

President Trump's personal lawyer, Jay Sekulow, *left*, arrives at the Capitol during the impeachment trial.

a Democrat representing Vermont.[3] One of the House managers, Demings, explained that the aid was released only after another Senate vote.

Following the questions, the senators again debated whether to call witnesses and admit additional evidence. On January 31, 2020, the Senate voted on this motion—51 against and 49 for.[4] No more evidence would be allowed before the final vote.

COMING TO THE END

At 9:00 p.m. on February 4, Trump gave his State of the Union address. As is the custom for all presidents, Trump discussed the state of the economy and the US military, as well as education and health care. He talked about

NO WITNESSES

For the most part, it was Republican senators who voted against bringing witnesses and additional evidence, in the form of documents, into the Senate trial. They gave several reasons for voting this down. First was the belief that it is the House's job to gather evidence, and if the representatives didn't gather enough, they should have waited until they had more to bring the case to the Senate. Senate Republicans also said that House Democrats should have tried harder to get the testimony they needed, compelling witnesses if necessary by issuing subpoenas instead of waiting until the trial opened in the Senate. Senate Republicans said they wanted to avoid potentially drawing the trial out for months. House Democrats said part of the reason they did not issue subpoenas was because they had also feared using a lengthy legal battle to pull witnesses, especially Bolton, in to testify. In every preceding impeachment trial, including those of President Andrew Johnson and President Bill Clinton, the Senate called in witnesses.

TRUMP AND PELOSI

When Trump gave his State of the Union address in the House Chamber, he and Nancy Pelosi exchanged slights starting the moment the president walked up to the House rostrum, the raised platform at the front of the chamber. Trump stepped up and handed Pelosi a copy of his speech, and she held out her hand to shake his in greeting, but he turned his back on her. When the time came for Pelosi to introduce the president, the typical introduction is, "I have the high privilege and distinct honor of presenting to you the president of the United States." Instead, she gave a much shorter introduction: "Members of Congress, the president of the United States." At the end of Trump's speech, Pelosi, who was seated behind Trump, held her copy of the speech up in view of the cameras and ripped the copy in half. She later told reporters she had done this "because it was a manifesto of mistruths."[5]

job growth, prayer in schools, and paid medical leave. The partisan divide was clear during the speech, with Republicans frequently applauding while Democrats sat silently. Trump did not mention the impeachment, though the vote on whether he would be convicted was scheduled for the next day. If convicted, he could be removed from office.

On February 5, 2020, the Senate voted first on the charge that Trump had abused the power of his office in getting a foreign power to investigate a political rival. One by one, each senator stood and stated his or her vote, either to convict or acquit. It was a tense moment. The Democrats held 45 out of 100 seats in the Senate, with 53 of the remaining seats held by Republicans and two by Independents.

A vote of 51 would be required to convict Trump of a charge. A vote of 67 on either charge would have both convicted him and removed him from office. In the end, the vote on the abuse of power charge was only 48 to convict and 52 to acquit. The vote on the charge of obstructing Congress was 47 to convict and 53 to acquit.[6] The president was cleared of both charges and remained in office.

BREAKING RANKS

Senator Mitt Romney, a Republican representing Utah, voted against the second article of impeachment, disagreeing that President Trump had obstructed Congress. But Romney broke with his party to vote for the first article of impeachment. Each senator was allowed to speak for up to ten minutes. Romney spoke of his faith and of his constitutional duty. He called Trump's behavior grievously wrong. "I will tell my children and their children that I did my duty to the best of my ability, believing that my country expected it of me," he said from the floor. "There's no question in my mind that were their names not Biden, the president would never have done what he did," Romney said in an eight-minute speech delivered in a Senate chamber that was nearly devoid of his colleagues.[7] Later, he added: "Corrupting an election to keep oneself in office is perhaps the most abusive and destructive violation of one's oath of office that I can imagine."[8] Democrats hailed his vote as courageous while the president's son, Donald Trump Jr., called for Romney's expulsion from the Republican Party.

FROM THE HEADLINES

VOTING ALONG PARTY LINES

Democrats and Republicans in both the House and Senate tend to vote along party lines. This can be seen in several key votes that took place throughout the impeachment process. At the time these votes were taken, the party breakdown in the House of Representatives was 232 Democrats, 196 Republicans, and one Independent, and in the Senate it was 45 Democrats, 53 Republicans, and two Independents.[9]

HOUSE VOTES ON ARTICLES OF IMPEACHMENT[10]

ARTICLE I: ABUSE OF POWER

230 YES, 197 NO, 1 PRESENT

ARTICLE II: OBSTRUCTION OF CONGRESS

229 YES, 198 NO, 1 PRESENT

SENATE VOTE ON ALLOWING ADDITIONAL EVIDENCE AND WITNESSES DURING TRIAL[11]

51 NO, 49 YES

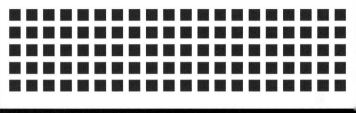

SENATE IMPEACHMENT TRIAL VOTES[12]

ARTICLE I: ABUSE OF POWER

52 ACQUIT, 48 CONVICT

ARTICLE II: OBSTRUCTION OF CONGRESS

53 ACQUIT, 47 CONVICT

CHAPTER NINE

MOVING
FORWARD

resident Trump was acquitted of the charges against him, which meant he would continue to serve as president. And, although an impeachment cannot be reversed, a January 2020 Gallup poll reported Trump's approval rating had risen. The poll, taken from January 16–29, 2020, showed Trump had a 49 percent approval rating, which was the highest it had been since he took office in 2017. He had a 94 percent approval rating among Republicans polled and 42 percent approval among Independents, compared with 7 percent among Democrats.[1]

Whether Trump's increased approval rating was a direct result of the impeachment is unknown, but it follows the trend seen during Bill Clinton's

Trump talks to reporters about his acquittal with First Lady Melania Trump at his side.

impeachment. When Clinton was impeached, his approval rating rose to 73 percent, a personal high for President Clinton.[2] The spike occurred after the impeachment vote in the House and continued through the Senate hearings and his acquittal.

Still, other factors could have fed into Trump's higher rating. Early on January 3, 2020, a US drone strike killed Iranian general Qassim Suleimani. He was Iran's most powerful security and intelligence commander, responsible for the killing of hundreds of US soldiers in the Iraq War (2003–2011). Fifty-three percent of those polled said that they approved of this action, while 45 percent disapproved.[3] American confidence in the economy was also the highest it had been in twenty years, a feeling that usually reflects well on the president's approval ratings.

BENEFITS FOR THE REPUBLICAN PARTY?

When Clinton was impeached, approval ratings for his party, the Democrats, remained at a high of 57 to 58 percent as measured in two December 1998 polls. While this shows the Democratic Party holding steady even when Clinton was impeached, the Republican Party's approval rating during Trump's impeachment rose from 43 percent in September 2019 to 51 percent in February 2020.[4]

EFFECT ON CAMPAIGNS

The impeachment affected the 2020 presidential campaign. As with any presidential race, heated debate had surrounded Trump's reelection campaign, and he wasn't shy about combating with Democrats. In a January 2020 political rally, President Trump said, "They can't win an election, so they're trying to steal an election."[5] But Trump was the first president to campaign for reelection after being impeached, and this was something Democrats would try to use in their favor. Biden came through the

While some voters supported the president, others were upset by the results of the impeachment trial.

impeachment relatively unscathed as far as Democratic voters were concerned. The former vice president later secured the 2020 Democratic Party nomination for the presidential election.

The impeachment intensified the battle for seats in Congress as well. Thirty-five Senate seats were up for votes the following November. Twenty-four were held by Republicans. The Democrats needed to pick up only four more seats to become the Senate majority. Republicans running for office in 2020 reminded voters of the Democrats' failed attempt at removing Trump from office. Democratic candidates would defend what was accomplished in the House, as voters who supported the impeachment were disappointed when Trump was acquitted. A few seats won or lost in either house of Congress could cause a shift in political power in the legislative branch, and candidates would make an effort to attract swing voters.

> "HOUSE DEMOCRATS RISK A VOTER BACKLASH DUE TO THE PERCEPTION THAT THEY INVESTED THEIR ENTIRE MAJORITY ON IMPEACHMENT, GETTING ALMOST NOTHING ELSE DONE."[6]
>
> —POLITICAL CONSULTANT MATT MACKOWIAK, 2020

REMOVING PERSONNEL

Just two days after President Trump was acquitted, two of the witnesses, Vindman and Sondland, were fired. Alexander Vindman was escorted out of the White House by security, as was his twin brother, Yevgeny Vindman, a senior lawyer and ethics official on the National Security Council. When asked about his feelings for Alexander Vindman, Trump was clear. "I'm not happy with him. You think I'm supposed to be happy with him?" he said.[7] Shortly after the Vindmans were removed, Sondland was fired from his ambassadorship.

Throughout his presidency, Trump had shown a demand for loyalty, particularly within his administration, where he frequently made personnel changes to remove people he no longer trusted. The impeachment seemed to strengthen Trump's emphasis on loyalty. The White House Office of Presidential Personnel is responsible for evaluating thousands of political appointees. Not long after Trump was acquitted, the office's director, John McEntee, held a meeting with liaisons from the various cabinets in Trump's administration. McEntee asked them to identify government staff members who might be disloyal to the president.

Impeachment-related dismissals continued when on April 3, 2020, Trump fired Inspector General Michael Atkinson. Atkinson, as inspector general of the intelligence community, was the person who brought the whistleblower's complaint about the phone call with Zelensky to the House Intelligence Committee. In a letter to both the House and Senate Intelligence Committees, Trump said that he no longer had confidence in Atkinson.

It was hard to say what the long-term effects of the impeachment would be. The president's post-impeachment increase in popularity failed to last, dropping to 43 percent approval by April 1, 2020, amid concerns over the administration's handling of an intensifying global pandemic.[8] But it seemed clear there

Trump holds up a newspaper announcing his acquittal.

would be some impact as discussions surrounding the
2020 election continued.

The impeachment of President Donald Trump marked
only the third presidential impeachment in US history,
and for months it thrust the stark ideological divisions
among the primary political parties into the public eye. It
underscored the importance of the Constitution's checks
and balances, which allow the most powerful leaders to
be held accountable but also provide protections for those
leaders. Analysis of the impeachment and its ramifications
will influence the country's development for years
to come.

ESSENTIAL
FACTS

MAJOR EVENTS

- On September 20, 2019, the *Wall Street Journal* runs a news story about a July 25, 2019, phone call between President Donald Trump and the new Ukrainian president, Volodymyr Zelensky. Witnesses said Trump had pushed for Zelensky to investigate Hunter Biden, the son of Trump's political rival Joe Biden.

- After investigating the phone call, on December 18, 2019, the House of Representatives votes to impeach President Trump for abuse of power and obstruction of Congress.

- The Senate tries President Trump, ultimately voting to acquit him on February 5, 2020.

KEY PLAYERS

- President Donald Trump was impeached in 2019 in relation to accusations that he tried to persuade a foreign government to investigate former vice president Joe Biden and his son Hunter Biden.

- Ukrainian president Volodymyr Zelensky was allegedly asked by Trump to investigate the Bidens.

- Former vice president Joe Biden, as he sought the Democratic bid for the 2020 presidential election, was discussed during Trump's questioned phone call with Ukraine.

- House Speaker Nancy Pelosi led the House Democrats through the impeachment process.

- Representative Adam Schiff, a Democrat from California, was the chair of the House Intelligence Committee and a lead investigator in the impeachment.

IMPACT ON SOCIETY

The impeachment of President Donald Trump encouraged Republican voters who felt that their president had emerged victorious. These Republicans had put Trump in office, and the Democrats were unable to remove him. Meanwhile, some Democratic voters found themselves disappointed. Despite the Republican majority in the Senate, many Democrats had hoped for a different outcome. And people across all political parties were able to reflect on the information brought forward in the impeachment hearings, whether they felt it proved Trump trustworthy or corrupt.

QUOTE

"We know how it's going to end. There is no chance the president is going to be removed from office."

—Senate Majority Leader Mitch McConnell, 2019

GLOSSARY

ACQUIT
To clear a person of the charges that have been brought against him or her.

AMBASSADOR
A person who is an official representative for a country in its relationships with other countries.

AMENDMENT
A formal addition or change to a document or law.

CABINET
A group of people whose job is to advise the head of a government, such as a president.

COLLUSION
Secret cooperation for illegitimate or illegal purposes.

CONFIDENTIAL
Secret.

CONVICT

To find a person guilty of criminal charges.

CORRUPT

Acting in a dishonest way; this term is often used to describe political figures.

DEPOSITION

Legally binding testimony.

INTELLIGENCE COMMUNITY

The collection of separate US government agencies that collect information to support national security.

PROSECUTOR

A legal official who charges people with criminal offenses and argues for the charges in court.

SERVER

A computer in a network that is used to provide services to other computers in the network.

SUBPOENA

An official written command that summons a person to appear in court.

ADDITIONAL
RESOURCES

SELECTED BIBLIOGRAPHY

Nadler, Jerrold. "Impeachment of Donald J. Trump, President of the United States. Report of the Committee on the Judiciary, House of Representatives." *House of Representatives*, 13 Dec. 2019. docs.house.gov. Accessed 30 Apr. 2020.

"Read: Republican Report on the Impeachment Inquiry." *NPR*, 2 Dec. 2019. npr.org. Accessed 30 Apr. 2020.

"Read Trump's Phone Conversation with Volodymyr Zelensky." *CNN*, 26 Sept. 2019. cnn.com. Accessed 30 Apr. 2020.

FURTHER READINGS

Carser, A. R. *Donald Trump: 45th US President*. Abdo, 2017.

Hurt, Avery Elizabeth. *The United States Constitution*. Cavendish Square, 2018.

The Politics Book: Big Ideas Simply Explained. DK Publishing, 2018.

ONLINE RESOURCES

To learn more about the impeachment of Donald Trump, please visit **abdobooklinks.com** or scan this QR code. These links are routinely monitored and updated to provide the most current information available.

MORE INFORMATION

For more information on this subject, contact or visit the following organizations:

National Constitution Center
Independence Mall
525 Arch St.
Philadelphia, PA 19106
215-409-6600
The National Constitution Center offers exhibits about US history, government, and the Constitution.

U.S. Capitol Visitor Center
United States Capitol
Washington, DC 20510
202-226-8000
visitthecapitol.gov
The United States Capitol is where the members of Congress work. The visitor center includes exhibits to educate the public about the Senate and the House of Representatives, along with other historical exhibits.

SOURCE
NOTES

CHAPTER 1. "LET US IN!"

1. Ed Kilgore. "Republicans Storm Closed Meeting, Demanding Transparency for Their Stonewalling POTUS." *New York*, 23 Oct. 2019, nymag.com. Accessed 4 June 2020.

2. @RepMattGaetz. "BREAKING: I led over 30 of my colleagues into the SCIF where Adam Schiff is holding secret impeachment depositions. Still inside – more details to come." *Twitter*, 23 Oct. 2019, 10:32 a.m., twitter.com. Accessed 4 June 2020.

3. Meg Wagner, Veronica Rocha, Fernando Alfonso III, and Aimee Lewis. "The Latest on the Trump Impeachment Inquiry." *CNN*, 24 Oct. 2019, cnn.com. Accessed 4 June 2020.

4. Manju Raju and Jeremy Herb. "After Republicans Storm Hearing Room, Defense Official Testifies in Impeachment Inquiry." *CNN*, 23 Oct. 2019, cnn.com. Accessed 4 June 2020.

5. Li Zhou and Ella Nilsen. "House Republicans' Impeachment Stunt Is an Attempt to Distract from the Allegations against Trump." *Vox*, 23 Oct. 2019, vox.com. Accessed 4 June 2020.

6. Kilgore, "Republicans Storm Closed Meeting."

CHAPTER 2. WHAT IS IMPEACHMENT?

1. "Impeachment." *US Senate*, n.d., senate.gov. Accessed 4 June 2020.

2. "Impeachment."

3. Alicia Parlapiano. "How the Constitution Defines Impeachable, Word by Word." *New York Times*, 8 Dec. 2019, nytimes.com. Accessed 4 June 2020.

4. Parlapiano, "How the Constitution Defines Impeachable."

CHAPTER 3. THREATS AND INVESTIGATIONS

1. "2016 Presidential Election Investigation Fast Facts." *CNN*, 31 May 2020, cnn.com. Accessed 4 June 2020.

2. Michael Crowley and Tyler Pager. "Trump Urges Russia to Hack Clinton's Email." *Politico*, 27 July 2016, politico.com. Accessed 4 June 2020.

3. "The 2016 US Presidential Election." *History.com*, 5 Aug. 2019, history.com. Accessed 4 June 2020.

4. Susan Heavey. "Trump Seeks to Backtrack on 2017 Comments on Comey Firing." *Reuters*, 30 Aug. 2018, reuters.com. Accessed 4 June 2020.

5. James Griffiths. "Trump Says He Considered 'This Russia Thing' before Firing FBI Director Comey." *CNN*, 12 May 2017. Accessed 4 June 2020.

6. "IG Footnotes: Serious Problems with Dossier Sources Didn't Stop FBI's Page Surveillance." *Chuck Grassley*, 15 Apr. 2020, grassley.senate.gov. Accessed 4 June 2020.

CHAPTER 4. IMPEACHMENT INQUIRY

1. "Read Trump's Phone Conversation with Volodymyr Zelensky." *CNN*, 26 Sept. 2019, cnn.com. Accessed 4 June 2020.

2. "Ukraine, Nuclear Weapons, and Security Assurances at a Glance." *Arms Control Association*, July 2017, armscontrol.org. Accessed 4 June 2020.

3. "Read Trump's Phone Conversation with Volodymyr Zelensky."

4. "Fact Check: White House Legal Argument against Impeachment Inquiry." *NPR*, 9 Oct. 2019, npr.org. Accessed 4 June 2020.

5. "Trump Impeachment: Pelosi Launches Inquiry into Ukraine Claims." *BBC News*, 25 Sept. 2019, bbc.com. Accessed 4 June 2020.

6. "Trump Impeachment."

7. "Trump Impeachment."

8. "How People across the US Are Reacting to Trump's Call with the Ukrainian President." *NPR*, 26 Sept. 2019, npr.org. Accessed 4 June 2020.

CHAPTER 5. PUBLIC HEARINGS

1. Susan Davis. "House Will Vote to Formalize Impeachment Procedures in Ongoing Inquiry." *NPR*, 28 Oct. 2019, npr.org. Accessed 4 June 2020.

2. Davis, "House Will Vote to Formalize Impeachment Procedures."

3. Davis, "House Will Vote to Formalize Impeachment Procedures."

4. Veronica Rocha, Mike Hayes, Meg Wagner, and Bianca Britton. "The Latest on the Trump Impeachment Inquiry." *CNN*, 29 Oct. 2019, cnn.com. Accessed 4 June 2020.

5. Rocha et al., "The Latest on the Trump Impeachment Inquiry."

6. Peter Baker and Michael D. Shear. "Key Moments from the Impeachment Inquiry Hearing." *New York Times*, 21 Nov. 2019, nytimes.com. Accessed 4 June 2020.

7. Veronica Rocha and Meg Wagner. "Two Key Impeachment Witnesses Testify." *CNN*, 21 Nov. 2019, cnn.com. Accessed 4 June 2020.

8. Michael D. Shear. "Key Moments from Hill and Holmes's Testimony in the Impeachment Inquiry." *New York Times*, 21 Nov. 2019, nytimes.com. Accessed 4 June 2020.

9. "Transcript: The Witnesses: Gordon Sondland." *NBC News*, 21 Nov. 2019, nbcnews.com. Accessed 4 June 2020.

10. Michael D. Shear. "Key Moments from the First Impeachment Hearing in the Judiciary Committee." *New York Times*, 5 Dec. 2019, nytimes.com. Accessed 4 June 2020.

11. Shear, "Key Moments from the First Impeachment Hearing in the Judiciary Committee."

SOURCE NOTES CONTINUED

12. Shear, "Key Moments from the First Impeachment Hearing in the Judiciary Committee."

13. Richie Duchon and Alex Johnson. "House Judiciary Committee Publishes Full Impeachment Report." *NBC News*, 16 Dec. 2019, nbcnews.com. Accessed 4 June 2020.

CHAPTER 6. ARTICLES OF IMPEACHMENT

1. "Read Nancy Pelosi's Remarks on Articles of Impeachment." *New York Times*, 5 Dec. 2019, nytimes.com. Accessed 4 June 2020.

2. Grace Segers, Kathryn Watson, Stefan Becket, and Victoria Albert. "Judiciary Committee Ends Debate on Impeachment Articles." *CBS News*, 13 Dec. 2019, cbsnews.com. Accessed 4 June 2020.

3. Segers et al., "Judiciary Committee Ends Debate on Impeachment Articles."

4. Segers et al., "Judiciary Committee Ends Debate on Impeachment Articles."

5. Segers et al., "Judiciary Committee Ends Debate on Impeachment Articles."

6. Adam Entous. "Will Hunter Biden Jeopardize His Father's Campaign?" *New Yorker*, 1 July 2019, newyorker.com. Accessed 4 June 2020.

7. "Here's How the House Voted on Trump's Impeachment." *Politico*, 18 Dec. 2019, politico.com. Accessed 4 June 2020.

8. Sean Collins. "Rep. Tulsi Gabbard Explains Why She Voted 'Present' on the Articles of Impeachment." *Vox*, 18 Dec. 2019, vox.com. Accessed 4 June 2020.

9. Segers et al., "Judiciary Committee Ends Debate on Impeachment Articles."

10. Chris Cillizza. "It's Ken Starr vs. Ken Starr on Impeachment." *CNN*, 28 Jan. 2020, cnn.com. Accessed 4 June 2020.

CHAPTER 7. PREPARING FOR TRIAL

1. "The Impeachment Process in the Senate." *Congressional Research Service*, 21 Jan. 2020, crsreports.congress.gov. Accessed 18 Mar. 2020.

2. Bob Fredericks. "Chief Justice John Roberts Sworn in for Trump's Impeachment Trial." *New York Post*, 16 Jan. 2020, nypost.com. Accessed 4 June 2020.

3. "Trial Memorandum of President Donald J. Trump." *Just Security*, 20 Jan. 2020, justsecurity.org. Accessed 4 June 2020.

4. "Impeachment Trial Brief and Response." *YaleGlobal Online*, n.d., yaleglobal.yale.edu. Accessed 4 June 2020.

CHAPTER 8. TRIAL AND ACQUITTAL

1. Siobhan Hughes. "After Marathon Session, Senate Passes Trump Impeachment Trial Rules." *Wall Street Journal*, 22 Jan. 2020, wsj.com. Accessed 4 June 2020.

2. Carl Hulse. "Why Block Impeachment Witnesses? Republicans Have Many Reasons." *New York Times*, 30 Jan. 2020, nytimes.com. Accessed 4 June 2020.

3. "Trial of Donald J. Trump, President of the United States." *Congressional Record Online*, n.d., congress.gov. Accessed 4 June 2020.

4. Christina Wilkie and Yelena Dzhanova. "Senate Votes against Calling New Witnesses in Trump's Impeachment Trial." *CNBC*, 31 Jan. 2020, cnbc.com. Accessed 4 June 2020.

5. Cheryl Gay Stolberg. "Trump and Pelosi Exchange Snubs at the State of the Union Address." *New York Times*, 4 Feb. 2020, nytimes.com. Accessed 4 June 2020.

6. Seung Min Kim. "In Historic Vote, Trump Acquitted of Impeachment Charges." *Washington Post*, 6 Feb. 2020, washingtonpost.com. Accessed 4 June 2020.

7. Dan Balz and Robert Costa. "Romney Votes to Convict Trump on Charge of Abuse of Power, Becomes the Lone Republican to Break Ranks." *Washington Post*, 5 Feb. 2020, washingtonpost.com. Accessed 4 June 2020.

8. Kim, "In Historic Vote, Trump Acquitted of Impeachment Charges."

9. "Member Information/Congressional Profile." *House of Representatives Office of the Clerk*, n.d., clerk.house.gov. Accessed 4 June 2020.

10. Jacob Pramuk and John W. Schoen. "Here's How Each House Member Voted on the Impeachment of President Trump." *CNBC*, 19 Dec. 2019, cnbc.com. Accessed 4 June 2020.

11. Kyle Cheney, John Bresnahan, and Andrew Desiderio. "Republicans Defeat Democratic Bids to Hear Witnesses in Trump Trial." *Politico*, 31 Jan. 2020, politico.com. Accessed 4 June 2020.

12. Veronica Rocha, Mike Hayes, Meg Wagner, and Fernando Alfonso III. "Trump Acquitted at Impeachment Trial." *CNN*, 6 Feb. 2020, cnn.com. Accessed 4 June 2020.

CHAPTER 9. MOVING FORWARD

1. Jeffrey M. Jones. "Trump Job Approval at Personal Best 49%." *Gallup*, 4 Feb. 2020, news.gallup.com. Accessed 13 Mar. 2020.

2. Jones, "Trump Job Approval at Personal Best 49%."

3. Jones, "Trump Job Approval at Personal Best 49%."

4. Jones, "Trump Job Approval at Personal Best 49%."

5. Michael Collins and Rebecca Morin. "The Trial Is Over. Trump Won. Now Get Ready for the Political Fallout." *USA Today*, 6 Feb. 2020, usatoday.com. Accessed 4 June 2020.

6. Collins and Morin, "The Trial Is Over."

7. Karen Freifeld. "Two Days after His Acquittal, Trump Ousts Two Star Impeachment Witnesses." *Reuters*, 7 Feb. 2020, reuters.com. Accessed 19 Mar. 2020.

8. "Trump Job Approval." *Gallup*, n.d., news.gallup.com. Accessed 17 Apr. 2020.

INDEX

ABOUT THE
AUTHOR

SUE BRADFORD EDWARDS

Sue Bradford Edwards is a Missouri nonfiction author who writes about society and history. She is the author or coauthor of 20 other titles from Abdo Publishing, including *The Murders of Tupac and Biggie*, *The Assassination of John F. Kennedy*, and *Hidden Human Computers*. At her house, dinners before an election are full of conversation as each person tries to win everyone else over to his or her chosen candidate.